It Could Be Verse

Clive Oseman

Black Eyes Publishing UK

It Could Be Verse
By Clive Oseman
© Clive Oseman, 2020

Published by Black Eyes Publishing UK, 2020
Brockworth, Gloucestershire, England
www.blackeyespublishinguk.co.uk

ISBN: 9781913195090

Clive Oseman has asserted his moral right under the Copyright, Designs and Patents Act, 1988, to be identified as the author of this work.

All Rights reserved. No part of this publication may be reproduced, copied, stored in a retrieval system, or transmitted, in any form or by any means, without the prior written consent of the copyright holder, nor be otherwise circulated in any form of binding or cover other than that in which it is published and without a similar condition being imposed on the subsequent purchaser.

A CIP catalogue record for this title is available from the British Library.

Cover design: Jason Conway, cre8urbrand.
www.cre8urbrand.co.uk

It Could Be Verse is my third collection, and the one of which I am by far the most proud, with a pretty even split between humorous and serious material.

I have many people to thank for making it possible - too many to mention if I want to make room for the poems - so, if you have helped me in any way please realise that I appreciate it and that I thank you too.

Special thanks go to the following people, in no particular order:

Nick Lovell, who has been a great friend since a chance meeting back in 2014 and has helped me every step of the way, as well as being my co-host at Oooh Beehive.

Chloe Jacquet, whose help and advice have been invaluable. It's a huge advantage when one's favourite poet is a friend who is always willing to help by reading and giving honest, but always diplomatic, feedback.

Everyone involved in the Gloucestershire Poetry Society, especially Ziggy Slug, Jason Conway, Josephine Lay and Peter Lay.

Everyone who has supported Oooh Beehive.

Anyone who has had enough faith in me to book me to perform at their events.

Away from the spoken word scene, a special thank you to Katie Webb, a treasured friend of long standing, who has always believed in me when sometimes I haven't believed in myself.

As always, I dedicate the book to my daughter Germaine, who is never out of my thoughts.

It Could Be Verse

Contents

The A to Z of Animalz	9
It Could Be Worse	14
Ready To Compete	16
Talent Show	18
Poundland's Last Stand	20
Treadmill	22
Bad?	24
Open Mic	25
Second Chance	27
Difference	30
Vote For This Poem!	32
Flat White	34
Prisoner	36
See It, Say It, Sorted	38
The Way It Is	41
In Celebration of National Poetry Day (2018)	43
Simple	44
Your Song	47
Equilibrium	49
The Queen's Abdication Honours List	50
A Special Grandad	52
Misrepresentation	54
Journey	56
Arson	57
The Poet	58
Doomsday	60
My Spade Will Always Be A Spade	62
New Year's Eve (2019)	65
Alien Interview	66
If Typos Had Consequences	70

The A to Z of Animalz

Aardvark appears
ahead of absolutely all else,
the apex of alphabetical arrangement.
Some alternative animals are agitated,
acrimonious or even apoplectic
although a few are actually ambivalent.

Bison, being bolshie,
bemoan every bit of bloody bullshit
being bunged at them.
Brainy, but belittled because their breed
sounds like 'basin' in broad Brummie,
the big buggers are bothered by bullying,
but blasé about Brexit.

Conversely, cats are casually content
'cause they can't comprehend or care
about concepts categorising creatures
as they carelessly claw chunks
from the cutis of Clarissa.

Dogs demand different definitions.
Don't dare diss Dalmatians or Dobermans.
Doing dem down is downright dangerous,
dallying with disaster, dicing with death.
Don't do it!

Every elephant eats enormously,
is easy going over extraneous elements
and etymology.
Some endure ears even more excessive
than my extraordinary eyesores.

Foxes are furious.
Forever affiliated with fake 'facts'
fanks to that fascist fart's favourite
fuckwittery-flinging faecal fiction factory,
Fox news,
they feel fully fucked over by fate.

Giraffes go gazing over gigantic gates,
getting glimpses of gloriously gorgeous greenery.
Grandma giraffes gasp and go gaga
for glamorous Gary, the great
ginormous gigolo of giraffedom.

Humans, horrifically heartless,
hold heavy-handed influence on the hereafter.
Has anything any hope?
Heaven help the helpless as our habitat
hovers on a holocaust.

Impalas, iguanas.
Idle rhyme in iambic lines.
In fact, immensely incompatible.
It's irrational imagining interspecies intercourse.
Idiotic idea!

Jellyfish just take joy in jeopardising
enjoyment of jolly seaside jaunts.
Jackass jerks! Jeez, jellyfish. Just...?

Kangaroos can kick in a kerfuffle.
Kevin was killed by a king-size kanga,
keeled over after a kick in the knackers.
Probably Karma. Kevin was a knucklehead.

Loveable llamas live longish lives.
Adam the llama is ludicrously lucky
and earns lots of lolly playing for Liverpool
living in luxury, however unlikely.

Meerkats are members of the mongoose family.
Magnificent, memorable, meek,
mild mannered and matey,
yet multiple meerkats make a mob.
Many make money
measuring the merits of markets.

Nightingales are notable for singing nicely.
Now, new evidence
names nightingale songs as nakedly noxious
in their nature, never neglecting nastiness
and nearly nihilistic.
In a nutshell, our notion of the nature
of the nightingale has been naïve.
They need the nourishment of notoriety.

Ocelots oscillate between
outrageously obnoxious and out and out ordinary.
Only occasionally observably obvious,
one once openly organised ocelot orgies
in zoos near Oldham and Ormskirk.

Pity poor Percy Polecat,
perpetrating powerfully pernicious pongs
projecting poor perceptions of Percy
and producing puking from people.

Q. Hmmm
Quagga, quetzal, quokha.
Qwyst Almighty! Quite a quandary.
Quality over quantity.
Quickly quashing Q.

Roland Rat's revolting.
Roger Rabbit's reproducing.
Rudolph the red nosed reindeer.
Rocky raccoon.
Rhinos rarely read romance
to relax on railways.

Squirrels are stupid.
Syril the squirrel sometimes seems sensible
then says something silly,
suggesting some sort of shortcoming
in syntactical skills
and substandard schooling.

Then there's the tangerine-textured tosspot,
totally tactless, toxic tyrant.
Timber-brained, temper-tantrum trendsetter
to the terrible twos.
Trashy Trump.

Upupa epops. Upupa? u pupa.
Use usuperdooperpooperscooper.
Undeniably unique.

Vicunas. Very, very, very fast.
Vanish at velocity. Vroom.
Victory for wisdom versus valour.

Wallabies wannabe wonderful.
Well, who or what wouldn't?
I wish I was a wizard
waving wands at woes.
Wish away, wallaby wankers.

Xanthareel, xantis, xantu, xenons,
xenarthra, xerus, xiphosuran.
All x-rated, xtremely awkward
xylophone playing, xerox copying, xenophobes
to make Xavier X-asperated!

Yaks of yesteryear yearned to learn to yodel.
Yes, efforts yielded tiny yaps
and yelps that travelled yards,
yet yaks are yet to yodel.
Young yaks do yoga instead.

Zebras are ztripey, not zigzagged.
Zoom in on Zelda driving a Zephyr,
zipping away from the zoo,
Zelda's zister, Zoe Zebra zonked out
catching Zs.

zzzzzzzz

It Could Be Worse

I'm not suggesting my life's a mess
but if it were a game of chess
the bishop has probably just confessed
to sideways moves brought on by stress,
the queen's been kneeling, praying for a
divorce from the Duke of Edinburgh.
The rooks think they're castles
the knights are moody
the pawns have all just made a movie
and the king is actually a prince
who has waited so long it's sent him loopy.

I'm not saying I fucked up in style
but life's like a show by Jeremy Kyle
in that I've been a prick for quite a while
yet only now am I reviled.
But, hey, I've still got a career
not based on verbal diarrhoea,
responsible for suicide
after branding people cheats and thieves,
feckless scum and paedophiles,
with a worthless device for detecting liars.

So, if your life is like a horror pic
count your blessings for a bit.
At least it's not British politics,
trashed by clueless lunatics
obsessed with the ridiculous
superiority of Britishness.
A bunch of self-centred pricks
so cold and heartless they make me spit
as they turn a blind eye to starving kids
to make a quick buck out of Brexit.

Remember you're not one of them.
Hasn't that cheered you up a bit?

Ready To Compete

It's been a pretty good few days, all told.
A few problems solved
and I have told myself that
though the world hasn't turned to gold
some good things are about to unfold.

I'm not yet running but I'm on my feet,
not in retreat, and where I would often
just concede defeat
I now feel ready to compete,
to stand up and be counted,
hold my ground and without conceit
display the trace of hope that I have found.

I've learned we all have problems,
we all have doubts,
but when morale is heading south,
we can drown them out,
douse the flames of negativity,
blunt the edge of sensitivity
with a reminder of what life's about;
a series of ups and downs.

We will not drown on rainy days
but better appreciate the sun's rays
when they finally come our way.
There is always hope tomorrow
when today has had its say.

No one is immune from descending darkness.
The people you admire,
who are happy with their partners
or enjoying the freedoms of single life,

cannot see the pain you feel inside
but neither can you see what their smiles hide.

We all magnify our strife.
Some disguise it better than others
some smother it beneath the covers,

but show me someone always happy
and I'll show you deceit.
Their greatest feat is coping.
I'm not sure I've achieved that yet.
But there's nothing wrong with hoping.

Talent Show

This is my back story,
some would say my 'sob story'
my get to know me
my obligatory pity me
my spiel to make you vote for me.

Everything's dark.
The problems are coming two by two
like a Noah's ark of fucking shit.
I'm in recovery.
The music plays its part, does its bit,
as I say woe is me,
my singing is my therapy,
so vote for me. Score me high.
Do it each time until the crown is mine.
Vote multiple times on premium lines.

I've had a hard life,
each day a new knife in the back
for the man who once lived
on booze and crack.
I've given it the sack, but it wants me back.

Help me. Vote for me,
make me a celebrity.
My parents hate me
my singing is off key
my guitar playing is ropey
but once you get to know me,
well I'm an arsehole actually.

But don't let that stop you
because I want to be famous

and the shitshow is shameless enough
to build me up,
tell me they are very impressed,
then, when they've made enough
out of my growing success,
leak past misdemeanours to the press
and let the journos do the rest.

Endless publicity for the show
and more money rolling in
from the telephone
as people decide I've got to go
so they vote for the angel in disguise
who avoided the public diatribes.

The negative attention could destroy me
a downward spiral could embroil me
but it's a risk I am prepared to take.
I'm craving fame and wide acclaim
they're my drugs of choice
and the only hope is in my voice.
Think of the money I could make
if the praise they lavished wasn't fake.

Fame and fortune are all that matters.
Vote for me. My life's in tatters.

Poundland's Last Stand

I'm not the people's poet
but Poundland's last stand,
the half price 'Smartprice'
supermarket own brand,

panned by the landed and the grand
whose fans can't understand
why there would be demand
to listen to people like me.

I barely went to school, you see,
let alone the gilded halls and corridors
of establishment and privilege,
where money opens doors
for those whose wealth was
pillaged from the poor,

and impenetrable metaphors
based on ancient times and folklore
mean those "not in the club" are bored,
their rough and ready nature scorned.

Me? I'd rather listen to the youth
or people who can speak their truth
in real terms,
those from the grassroots who are influenced
by experience of no concern to those
who learned to wrap up words in fancy clothes.

I will always listen to what I can relate to,
use plain language to debate you
and maybe alienate you
with an expletive or two.

That doesn't mean I hate you,
or that I do not rate you,
but try tracing where I come from,
feeling what I've been through
and you may respect me too.
My grammar isn't perfect
my knowledge isn't deep
but people understand me
and those who show belief
can listen to what I have to say
and know I'm here for keeps.

Treadmill

When you're on the outside looking in
and long to be accepted,
searching for an entry point
but always intercepted;
the recurring realisation
that you're once again rejected
leaves your ego bruised and battered,
your confidence so dented.

The pain of shame can weigh you down
when you never feel embraced,
when you give your best and never rest
in pursuance of your quest.
You are tested and requested
to show they should invest,
give their time to someone who
they don't wish to address.

Eventually you question motives
and why you even try
when your destiny seems set in stone
to always be denied.
Your tears quickly multiply
when you're often vilified,
when you know it's a losing battle
to be reclassified.

Something deep inside you
is saying let it be
but you've never been a quitter
and you're searching for belief.
You can knock
until your knuckles bleed

you're never getting in
and once you can accept this
you will find a new beginning.

Force out a huge, defiant grin
and raise your middle finger,
tell them they can swivel
you don't need them any longer.

If they don't accept your presence now
they probably never will
but the loss is theirs, it isn't yours
if you don't fit their bill.
Let your light shine somewhere worthy
shower them with your skill.
All it takes is one step back
from an unforgiving treadmill.

There's a world out there just waiting
for you to prove the doubters wrong,
and you will know it instantly
when you've found where you belong.

The weight will lift, the shackles loosen
and freedom will be sweet.
As you learn to fly and they can't deny
the greatness of your feats,
they'll call for you to come back here,
at their table there's a seat.
It's up to you to call the shots.
The mission is complete.

Bad?

There's a piece of Burma within me.
The slice of wartime jungle
that drove a man to madness,
filled his later years
with the sadness of destruction.

I never knew my real father,
just the shadow of a man
turned bad by the horrors of war.
What he was like before I can never be sure,
though sadly his siblings held some clues.

Is my hatred aimed at him
or just what he became?
The version of the person,
who was barbarously broken,
was responsible for much.

Do I clutch at straws,
ignore the family flaws
and say it wasn't him?
Can I ever cut through consequence
and forgive?

Open Mic

I listen with intent
at another spoken word event,
then towards the end of a top-class night
a young woman takes the mic
and with spectacular verbal dynamite
displays the trauma of broken family life.
The impact of a father's actions,
strife caused to those caught in the crossfire
of a battle between parents
when love breaks down, respect expires.

In this case it seems clear
where the fault lies
as we become familiarised
with the depth and ugliness of scars,
the cost in broken hearts
of thoughtless disregard of obligations.

This situation sounds so different
to the one that's too familiar,
but I guess the pain is similar
for those who lost stability and hope
and now are left to cope
with years of pent up anger and frustration.

Emotions overwhelm me
as the notion of my blame tells me
that I could have done things better.

Words mingle with memory and doubt
as regrets shout their hatred
and I can find no clear way out.

I see my daughter standing there
in someone else's body,
words taking the shape of question marks
sharp enough to rip my mind apart.

What does she think of me?
What will she say?
She's an adult now but I still see the child
in whose development I never had a say.

I always told myself, one day she'll understand
that I never wanted her to move away
that I had a losing hand
which was impossible to play
and the winner is the one that gets their way.

But I told myself a lot of things
and this moment brings the realisation
that the place in which I stand today
is haunted by the past,
the ghosts of things that couldn't last
and I wait for condemnation.

As the poet takes her long ovation,
I hide the helplessness I feel inside,
feel relief that this was not my girl
and I didn't have to face the tide
of a sea of revelations.
But despite this very brief salvation
I drown in all the tears she's cried.

Second Chance

You are living with the spectre of bad choices,
tormented by visions of the past
and the shameful shadows that they cast.

You find yourself dismissed
by those who remember a younger you
or have only heard the stories,
who have missed the shift of emphasis
and still see only negatives.

First impressions last
and some will have you classed as trouble.
To win them over will be a struggle
and maybe they are lost forever,
not understanding your endeavour
to be a better model of yourself.

You were misguided,
but can take pride in rehabilitation,
how you rose above the stagnation
and alienation you once felt.
We only have to scratch the surface
to see that you have changed,
found a whole new frame of mind.

Now is the time to find some peace,
feel the freedom of release.
You can move beyond the pain
now you've tamed the flame of anger.
Acknowledge you were wrong,
show that you belong in better times,
that you are strong and not defined
by that under which you've drawn a line.

It's true, a leopard never changes spots,
but who said you're a leopard?
Circumstances crafted the 'old' you.
You are not what you did, but what you do,
and those who won't give any due
for how far you have travelled
since it all unravelled,
have no clue, and don't deserve to know
the better version of you.

They can form a queue to offer apologies
when they realise your qualities.
It's certain they too made
serious errors of judgement
and should offer you encouragement.

Instead they jump to snap decisions,
misrepresent your mannerisms
and treat you with derision,
overlooking all their faults
on an ill-considered impulse.

Be that as it may
you are on your way to brighter days,
because in a world full of gloom
there is always room
for a light to shine.

You may not be water turned to wine,
no magic trick or miracle
but the new brand is authentic
so, aim for higher pinnacles.
You made mistakes and have repented,
to most, that's fine.
You've earned the chance to be respected

but it is to be expected
that some will have closed minds.

See this as a minor setback
on a long and winding path.

You are not in this alone.
Your failure was never set in stone
and there are plenty here to help you through,
to show the world what you can do.

How anyone can start anew.

Difference

Have you ever looked deep inside yourself
and seen down to the core?
Found pieces of your make up
which you can't help but abhor
side by side with those that you adore?

Some struggle with the latter,
spend a lifetime being battered
because their good doesn't fit the norm.
Hopefully, they learn never to conform,
the day dawns when they realise
what they were born to be
is not down to society
and being different does not mean
you are an anomaly.

Those who can't celebrate individuality
are denying their own fallibility
and are not a point of reference.
Their insistence that you don't belong
is merely their controlling song
designed to bend you to their will.

They aim to kill the real you
instil a version of themselves,
like we're mass produced
to be bought from shelves or off the peg,
not a powder keg of traits
that should never be up for debate.

I am a case in point.
Born to disappoint parents
of distorted vision,

raised in a dictatorial prison,
it took me decades to learn my lesson.
Thanks to them I'll never find anything
to love about myself
and nor will anyone else, I guess.
But I think this version of humanity
is better than what they tried to make me be
and I no longer hate those parts of me
that are not factory produced,
those that were traduced
by people knowing no better.

Our differences don't matter
in the way that our detractors preach.
We are who we are, and need no justification.

Take pleasure in their consternation
when you find the voice to speak.
We are each of us unique
and it's usually the weak who seek
to mould us in their image,
to hold us back and pillage
our world of opposition,
target insecurities with precision
to keep us in our place.

I realised all this far too late
so, if you feel you can relate,
rise up, don't listen to those
who will never understand.

You'll not find happiness
as someone else's brand.
Speak out, be proud, take flight.
Who knows where you will land?

Vote For This Poem!

This is a badly written poem
covered in the lustre of lies and false promise
and you're gonna love it.
It's gonna get your vote
as you note the slickness of the words
and overlook the sickness that is blurred
by the style with which I make it heard.

Poem means poem. Remember this.
So even if it scores fifty two percent
and in reality, makes no sense,
and you only scored it that high
because you were promised free entry
and sold pie in the sky,
I have to win.

There's no going back to the beginning
no chance to change your mind.
When you find it's full of bullshit lines
you're stuck forever with this poem of mine.
Your support was never binding
but the powers that be will be running scared.
Scared of upsetting me
and those who fell so foolishly
for my real lack of transparency.

This poem is shit.
and bit by bit it will destroy the scene.

I am the Farage of spoken word;
the Rees-Mogg, the Johnson, the absurd.
But it's the one that's best for me. Me. Me.
So, I broke the law, twisted democracy
to set you free of real poetry.

This is the future.
No McNish. No Hughes. No Tempest,
because you were impressed
when I promised you the best,
millions of masterpieces every week
to be read to help the old and weak.

And poetic democracy can't change its mind.
Even when sold a nursery rhyme.

Flat White

Having slipped outside for a quiet smoke,
I stepped back in, shared a joke
with the staff at my favourite coffee shop.
I sat at a table as the day slowly passed,
my third flat white at last boosting my senses,
speeding reflexes as the drowsiness
of all the late nights was effectively banished.

A young couple, clearly deeply in love,
passed the window
with their feelings setting light to the sky
the depth of affection
seen in the reflection of each other's eyes.
Then they vanished, like they never existed
except in my mind
or were blind to the real world
outside of their bubble.

A steady flow of traffic taking people away,
indicators winking at strangers in a bid for attention
were almost too humdrum to be worthy of mention.
But life's tapestry is remorselessly humdrum
and for some, such tedium is as good as it gets
except at weekends when with wildness released,
they get pissed or stoned
and the repulsive rigidity of routine is atoned.

It's alright for some!
I was sat sipping coffee
in my favourite place
with hours and hours and hours to waste.

Then came a sight that I'm not sure I liked.
A dog in the doorway, probably a stray
with a pink left eye and green speckled face.
This gave me a fright, but all it meant
is what I thought was a Woodbine
probably wasn't.
If the five purple paws didn't give it away
the way that he barked in immaculate French
and parked his car parallel to the fence
offered pretty substantial clues.

I thought this could well make the news,
a story to keep the nation amused
but then I think I must have passed out.

My body collapsed, it all headed south
and I bashed my face in
and knocked all my teeth out.

People say I look better like that.

And one thing I've learned, to my utter delight.
I get inspired to write when I'm high as a kite.

Prisoner

I could almost feel sorry for him
if only he realised how grim
and unforgiving his world can be
and tried to change things from within.

But he doesn't and he never will.
His mind's forever standing still,
imprisoned by the isms
he was brainwashed with,
destined to let his vision of the world
be tainted by the prejudice
that played a large part in his upbringing.

He maintains the family loathing of difference,
their insistence and persistence
in calling him to duty
resulting in a stunted personality
shunning individuality, reinforcing the banality
of the only life they knew.

How he makes them proud
spewing hatred in the loudest fashion.
displaying no compassion
no understanding of the multi-culture
enriching those around him,
unyielding to the rights of women,

wearing blinkers handed down
through generations,
refusing to remove them
even when the chance comes calling.

This is the age of the internet
with a world of information at your fingertips

and yet he chooses ignorance.
Refugees are scroungers,
Europeans have no right to grace these shores,
but he can travel where he likes
and his wife can bake the cakes
and do the chores.

We can blame his parents
for setting him on this course,
but the world is smaller now than it was for them
and they were never taught
any other strain of thought.

He chooses to be ignorant
out of hatred and resistance.
I could pity him, for sure
but forgive me for my reticence.
He's imprisoned by his isms.
But the key is there within his grasp
his sentence needn't last forever,
but it will.

He will always look back to the past
the glory days of Empire,
the privileges that are his of right
because he's male and he's white,
and feels they were stolen.

He will never see that equality is golden
that borders are a man-made concept
that flags and anthems forge contempt
that it's time white male dominance was spent.

I regret his refusal to tackle the issues he faces
but will never feel pity for misogynists or racists.

See It, Say It, Sorted

Everywhere you go these days
you hear the same old mantra replayed,
'If you see something that doesn't look right, report it
on 61016.
See it. Say it. Sorted.'

A palindromic cure to call
when you see anything wrong at all.
If only they were expeditious
whenever we did see something suspicious.

Things I could have reported for not looking right, include:
Swindon Town centre on a Saturday night,
full of Zombies who make Chris Grayling
look the type to get everything right.
I've seen the Queen address us near a gold piano
to royally take the piss.

I've seen two elderly walruses
arguing with venom
about which one of the pair of them
was actually John Lennon,
(I've been in rehab since)

But that's me being frivolous and slightly ridiculous
and I wouldn't expect meticulous investigations
because that's not what it's for.

Neither are the following
but I don't want them ignored
so, I see them, I say them. I do my best
but we have to join forces
to do the rest.

I see climate change deniers,
wealthy, self-centred liars
who claim it's all a myth,
that their dollars face no apocalypse,
while the Earth starts to burn
as it continues to turn,
but all that matters
is how much we can earn.

I see good people feared because they've been smeared,
with upholders of injustice being revered.

I see my country imploding
in xenophobic fervour,
controlling its borders and looking no further
than Folkestone or Dover.
The dream is over because British is best,
we've proved it before
with magnificent conquests and acts of war.
Nothing has changed, at least in the minds
of bigots who can't put the past behind them.

I see antisemitism on the rise,
Islamophobia rarely a surprise,
naked hatred in the eyes
of racists who refuse to realise
that the fact staring them in the face
is there is only one human race
and its very existence is on the line.

I see poor people being burned to death
because those with the money
took no steps to protect them,

then survivors still homeless after all this time
as billionaire's holiday homes stand unoccupied.
I see the Windrush generation being deported.

I see it. I say it. But fuck all gets sorted.

The Way It Is

I'm determined not to cry,
but today I'm asking why
and not finding any answers.

The physical pain I can accept -
it ravages and then lets go,
gives me a reprieve
and leads me to believe the worst is over.

It's not getting any worse,
it's quite the reverse
and if I look back twenty years or so
I know I'm lucky to be where I am.

I may be struggling right now
but that is how it is.
Next week, next month or sometime soon
it will change its tune,
play quietly in the background
as a barely audible sound,
with occasional loud bursts
to remind me it's around.

What I've found is, I accept this.
The constant attacks of years ago
that bound me to
the same four walls day in, day out,
unable to move without a hideous trigger
conditioned me to expect and accept a lifetime of it.
So, 'Bad today, OK tomorrow'
is a weird form of bliss.

What I'm struggling with is the other things;
the depression, the anxiety,
the sudden feelings of jeopardy.
The jumpiness, the sweats,
the tightness of the chest
when even the weight of a tee shirt
is an irritant.

The sleeplessness, broken only
by the nightmares, the flashbacks
the vividness of images
which linger for so long
it's almost like they're real.

The tiredness.
the feeling that I'm all alone
and willpower is the only asset I have.

The fear that just writing this
will intensify the loneliness
as people will steer clear.

But fuck it.
If you can't accept my weaknesses,
if you don't want to hear,
then I don't need you anywhere near.
So, feel free to disappear.

In Celebration of National Poetry Day (2018)

Today, we celebrated poetry.
Some used language romantic and flowery,
some got political, ranting
'Words will empower me.'
But of course they didn't
as some people wanted them locked up in prison
for crimes against metaphor. And dodgy rhythm.

Yet poetry was everywhere!
They erected a poet tree in Trafalgar Square.
I bought an artificial tree,
I don't want the dog choking on fallen simile.

People gave poetry cards as gifts to colleagues,
dismissing the hatred and office intrigue
and, 'Oh my word, wasn't I lucky?'
one had a verse by Carol Ann Duffy!

Then there were presents for kids.
If you gave the wrong poem, they'd never forgive.
Johnny wants a double acrostic sonnet
spelling 'Smash the system' and 'Kill capitalism.'
He's only eight, God bless him,
I don't want him disappointed.
It's bloody hard work but I'm already on it.

But no sooner the celebration came,
poetry was dismissed by the masses again.
Tomorrow, you see, is the fifth of October
National Poetry Day is over
and at tradition's pathetic insistence
we can all cream our pants
at the excitement of Christmas.

Simple

I wish I could be one of those people
happy with their lot, a simple outlook,
content with a closed book
of a life going nowhere.
Unconcerned by the wider world
because they like the hand they hold,
have a past to look back on
to protect them from the cold,
to stay with them until they're old,
and a bridge stretching back to those times
through the friends that they made,
who took similar journeys to be replayed
in their thoughts and talks on rainier days.

I wish I had done all the things
that so many take for granted,
that I wasn't the butt of the mirth
because I didn't get to do
what makes their memories
worth that little bit extra.

Do you remember...?
No, I don't.
Didn't you ever...?
No, I didn't
But you MUST have done this...?

I FUCKING DIDN'T!

That's what I feel like.
I want to scream. I want to shout.

NO! YOU'VE BEEN TOLD ENOUGH TIMES
SO SHUT YOUR FUCKING MOUTH!

But I don't.
I smile or laugh
because the joke's so funny
isn't it?

You DIDN'T?
Were you raised in the middle of nowhere
and kept in a box?

Tee hee,
I may as well have been.
But to say that ruins it all, you see.
What fun is there if I puncture your glee
by talking about the real me,
not the caricature you like to imagine.
So, feel free.
Take a low shot to get a cheap snigger
if it makes you feel any bigger.

The person that I am today
was manufactured in the yesterdays,
programmed with a lifetime of faults,
so that fucked up and lonely is my default.

Yes, I've made progress.
It's better than it used to be.
There's sticking plaster on the biggest scars,
and when people talk out of their arse
not knowing when they go too far,
I go along for the ride.

It's a matter of pride
not letting them see
how easily I come undone,
how much I want to hide.

Then when I slink away and sink
I think at least some people are aware
and kid myself that they may care.
Too soon, it seems
they've just forgotten that I'm there.

And I go on wishing I was one of those people
with a happy past to wear.

Your Song

Tell me all the things I have done wrong.
Sing the same old song
you've sung so many times
that all around you know it better
than they know their mind.

Spit it like the cheesy hits you learned
when you were young,
still repeating misheard lyrics
to make it your own song.

It doesn't matter that they're incorrect.
In your mind they connect,
and they're the only version
your loved ones know
so, their authenticity grows
as no one hears the original anymore.

Let's call it *Guilt Trip*.
Sing it to me for old time's sake,
see my morale dip to the depths
you've plunged me to so many times.
Remind me it was my mistake.

You're settling scores and I am bored,
too tired to fight, and ready to fall
under all the shovels of shit you've thrown at me
to keep your oh so righteous friends in thrall,
so, have it your way.
I have nothing more to say
and from today my hands are clean,
your dirty tactics washed away,

and the price you pay for this
will bankrupt you some day,
leave you nothing to fall back on
when people won't accept
the worthless currency of your words.

It will be too late for me,
but I will have moved on
away from your twisted fantasy
when you too lose the love of family.

My one request, when the hate begins...
Remember me when the pain kicks in.

Equilibrium

When I heard your voice I saw tomorrow
and your words carried the future
in the sweetness of their sound.
Time did cartwheels across my lines of thought
blurring boundaries between hope and truth,
unbalancing certainties in a whirlwind
of 'what ifs.'
Equilibrium has never been restored,
but the clocks have stubbornly stood still.

The Queen's Abdication Honours List

It is with the deepest of regret
that I have to announce
that I have set the date of my abdication.
I've been head of this nation for many years
and cringed at Phillip's aberrations
whenever he's escaped from the basement
to spew his views in public.

I've watched my children make bad choices
when left to their own devices
and now I'm old I'm gonna be bold
and go out with a bang,
buy Camilla some Polyfilla
and let Charles do his thang.

As it's time for one to step down and do less waving,
let God stop saving me and give him a King to worry about.
This is my abdication honours list,
I always reward those who have kissed my arse
or insignificant plebs who pass as representative of 'the masses',
like celebrity chefs or men who play in football matches,
people with dubious achievements. I like being mischievous.

So

A knighthood for Nigel Farage, for services to satire and xenophobia.
A Kinghood to Charlie boy
who'll briefly reign over ya with Queen Camilla.
(God knows I let him stew for long enough.

He's probably overcooked)
An OBE for Pete Doherty for services to high culture,
and a KFC for Jamie Oliver,
just to annoy him, for a bet.
A GCSE for Philip, for being a little dense.
A CBE and an OBE for Clive Oseman.
One for being so bloody hench,
the other for services to spoken word,
both equally well deserved.

And arise Sir Jacob Rees-Mogg
Who managed to unravel the mysteries of time travel
and become a modern-day Dickensian snob.

Now bugger orf peasants.
But feel free to help the aged
by sending me retirement presents.
I love you all you see,
and God, for saving me for so long,
in the words of that rather excellent song.
I wonder if he would accept a gong?

A Special Grandad

This man who was great at everything
with a charm and wit to make the birds sing,
you would want him with you in the trenches
he was the absolute master of all defences.
He'd bring the opposition to its knees,
they'd either die in battle or catch a terrible disease.
Go back to forty-four or so,
he fought the war and won it alone.

Before then he ruled the streets with fear,
a killer behind a respectable veneer.
If you didn't do what this man said
he'd beat you to death with a stale baguette
or a crusty bloomer about the head.
No knives or guns, he was too well bred.
He'd force feed you a poisoned scone,
the gentlemanly Al Capone.

He had magic powers to make things happen.
If he wanted to, he could break the pattern
of the sun going down and the sun coming up.
He could have made Birmingham win the Cup
(But the bastard didn't).
In his anger, when the bus didn't stop
he cursed so hard, its wheels fell off.

He was tougher than a rough pub's cheapest steak,
was immune to the venom of every snake.
He beat smallpox, chickenpox and, well, THE pox,
dysentery, malaria, the bends, and 'knob rot'.
Got knocked over and trashed the van.
Survived every illness known to man.

His charitable deeds knew no bounds,
he raised millions and millions and millions of pounds,
enthralled his sponsors and his fans
by walking to Moscow on his hands.

If you scored three then he scored four,
he was a concert pianist before he could walk.
Whatever you did he did better than that
so, to Grandad let's all raise our hats.

Because really when he lost our nan
he was just another lonely old man
who lived to tell us these tall tales
of how in his youth he never failed.

So, we let him grieve
and pretended to believe…
He fought in the war and won it alone,
the gentlemanly Al Capone,
when waiting for a bus that failed to stop
he cursed so hard its wheels fell off.
Survived every illness known to man
walked to Moscow on his hands.
Whatever you did he did better than that

and to Grandad we would raise our hats.

Then we buried him on a rainy Monday
and he rose like it was Easter Sunday
yelling 'OK you bastards, you can stop pretending.
My superpower is never ending.'

Misrepresentation

Magic is real, I'm told.
You can see it unfold
if you know what to look for
if you channel your thoughts
to the wavelength you ought to.

It's not a phenomenon that's new
it's existed through the ages
runs right through the pages of history
but to me, remains a mystery.

It isn't Paul Daniels or Dynamo.
When illusionists catch the eye,
you know they look better than reality,
that if you saw them with clarity
there's nothing special in their feats,
just deceit and suspension of disbelief.

It isn't the world of wizards and witches,
good versus evil and a child's upheaval
as portrayed in the barely believable tales
of the boy who lived,
the golden gift to the silver screen
where every supposedly suspense filled scene
led to a climax that all fans had foreseen.

The good guy won.
Because that's how it's done, right?
That's the magic of movies for sure.
We all go home cured of the blues
safe in the knowledge that good guys don't lose.

Magic powers like those found in fiction
or perfect performance by people
who have practiced for hours
misrepresent the meaning of the word.

It is simpler than that.
It is love and respect
reflected in actions of those we care for,
those we select to share life with
and the special bond of families.
The joy of living to bring up our kids.

I cannot confirm that it really exists.

Journey

Malevolent moods manipulate my mind
Emphasising everything erroneous.
Negative narratives nefariously nagging
To totally trash truth,
Aggressively attacking all assurances,
Leaving little likelihood of logic.

Hitting highs, hugging happiness,
Elevated. Ecstatic emotions easily
Abate again as an abyss approaches,
Light lost in loathsome loneliness,
Trapped in troubling, tunnelled thoughts.
Helpless to heal this hurt.

Arson

If you see or smell the fire
don't be disconcerted
or call the fire brigade.
This is no emergency.
Instead, join me
in dancing round the edges
bring the fuel and fan the flames.

It took a lot of courage
to strike the match
and watch the blaze take hold.

I want this out the way,
this comfort zone in which I alone
could sense the closing in of walls.

I need more space in which to stretch
and can't forget the thoughts
that were going through my head,

the nights I couldn't sleep,
the knowledge of the wasted chances
my own responsibility
for my circumstances.

Feel the heat. Let it burn
until I have no possible return.

The Poet

I'm inviting you to listen to
the truth about my writing,
how I'm fighting to be exciting
but will never be enlightening
because my stupidity is frightening.

I would run workshops
from Tavistock to Worksop
but my stock has dropped
because new ideas stopped
after all the rubbishy old ones flopped,
and my books were sold half price at Poundshop.

So, listen carefully to what I say
then run away down alleyways,
find yourself in a drunken haze,
smoke some dope with waifs and strays
then act on what your spaced-out muse says.

Because

Rhythm and rhyme hold sway with me
I let my mind run away with me
let the rhymes have their way with me,
hope that they will stay with me,
but write total bollocks unfailingly.

If alliteration is your titillation, I'm shit at it.
If you're into blank verse
then mine...could be worse,
because it's blank of all meaning,
has no depth of feeling,
is as empty as the public purse

in government speeches, well-rehearsed,
until the curse of war returns
and we have enough to put our kids in a hearse.

But that last verse is typical.
When the poetry's pitiful, get political
and like-minded people won't be too critical,
your insight will become almost mythical,
no one will be too analytical
as long as the rhymes don't get too difficult.

So find a target on the right
curse and swear with all your might
fill the audience with delight
with foul mouthed political dynamite,
and with luck they won't even realise
that actually, it's a crock of shite.

Doomsday

It's time we all faced up to it.
There's a proper risk of apocalypse.
The dreaded word is on our lips
as we're ready to tip off the edge of a cliff
and pledge the future to the demons
that await our rotting flesh with glee
and not a trace of decency.

You need to know the fight is lost,
it's closing in with every hour
and it's well beyond all human power
to prevent us all from being devoured.

This is not extremist politics,
or even the dreaded 'no deal' Brexit.
No, this is so much more apocalyptic.

We've been warned for months
how it would arrive,
how humanity would cease to thrive.
The signs have all been clearly there
but it seems as though we didn't care.

But now it's indisputable
the evidence irrefutable
so just in case you didn't know.
It's DEFINITELY going to SNOW!!!

It will mainly fall on higher ground
but even at lower altitudes
there'll be two or three millimetres
laying around with attitude.

This is your only chance to survive.
Get in your cars, go out and drive
and join the rush to panic buy.

Bread, milk and lots of tins,
cod liver oil and vitamins,
and don't forget your Easter eggs
and maybe even hot cross buns.

You may not be around on Easter day -
it is, after all, a few months away,
but freezing to death is not much fun
so, stuff your face, just in case.
Act quickly. The countdown has begun.

The mercury will plummet
and ice will form,
you'll wish you were in Benidorm.
But you're not. You're doomed
and your frozen flesh will be consumed.

In other news;
Man United managed a draw,
newspaper sales began to soar,
clickbait headlines denied the thaw,
as a brainwashed public
begged for more.

My Spade Will Always Be A Spade

What is poetry and spoken word to me?
What do I hope to achieve?
Do I need to get better
or do I just need something
in which to believe,
to be part of a scene?
Sometimes my writing, when personal,
is too much 'tell' and not enough 'show'.
I'm aware of this but it's OK though.
It'll win no accolades or awards
and I don't purport to be a superstar
but my words may strike a chord
with someone who needs to hear them.
I don't set puzzles,
because I want you to know,

I don't portray my father as a crow
and leave you to piece together
the meaning of the words,
then wonder if you really understood.
He was an abusive shit
and I've never once pretended
that my life didn't begin the day his ended.

My depression isn't a black dog
wanting to be stroked
and my physical pain is not personified
as a pissing alien controlling me.

I cope. I have a busy life,
and some don't like the way I tell it.
This is my soul
and I'm not about to sell it
to court approval from the purists.

My need to be loved
is not some curious concept
to be mollycoddled in metaphor.
Loneliness is a powerful word
that needs to be heard
because it's even more potent
if it goes unnoticed.
It feeds on itself
and gets ever more bloated.
I will tell my story as it is.
Raw and unpleasant,
from the ruined past up to the present.
If I'm a distant last in a poetry slam
then bollocks to it.
At least all those people know
exactly who I am.
I stood there with a mission
and accomplished it.
In my mind that makes me a winner.

To some I sound like a beginner
who never listened to the 'rules'
defining poetry to them.

A poem may be a flawless gem
to those inside the bubble,
but is it really worth the trouble
if it speaks in hushed, exclusive tones
and only ever reveals bare bones
to those with the right education?

What I do releases me,
unburdens me as I travel half a Nation
telling of my troubled past
or my current struggles.
Not everything I write is in this vein.

I'm not always talking grief and pain
but when I do, it fulfils a need.

I don't require perfect scores
in order to succeed
(Though they would of course
be very welcome indeed!)

I'm not the only abused child
who grew up fucked up,
I'm miles from being the only one with issues,
but it's better out than in,
especially if someone listening
can be inspired to find
they don't have to go through life
blind to the hidden path to
their redemption, to their desires
because they've found something
which lights their fires.

So, I'll be true to myself and stand defiant.

New Year's Eve (2019)

It's taken time, but the penny has dropped.
Time will never, has never, stopped
and if we settle only for what we've got
we just lose ground.
Happiness will never be found by looking back,
especially when the past lacked anything
that we could grasp and call our own,
when all the hopes that we have known
have died before they had a chance to grow.

This is the year that changed me,
made me see I can only be free
if I let go of toxicity,
step through the ever-open door
and leave behind the things I hoped for,
march towards a world that gives me more
than the failed dreams I had before.

It always hurts to admit defeat,
but it clears the path beneath our feet
and leads us to a different place,
where we've gained so much
but not lost face.

Alien Interview

Welcome to 'The World In Spotlight'.
I am privileged to be making history tonight.
Some listeners may well take fright
at what I'm about to reveal,
but that is alright, I feel.

It is understandable, indeed natural.
Some won't believe it is factual.
But it is.

I am thrilled to say that
what you will be hearing
is the first interview on Earth
with an alien being.

I have been warned
that due to the way translation is formed
this species bluntly speaks its mind
and may seem somewhat unrefined.
The technology is designed for the masses
from a planet that does not recognise 'classes'.

My first questions are these.
What is your name, where are you from,
and why have you decided to make contact?

unintelligible noise…

I cannot understand you…

*I'm sorry. I forgot to switch my translator
into Earthling English mode,
so, when the words flowed
you did not understand them.*

*It's easy to forget that without the gem
of universal understanding,
without translation on Earthling settings,
you stupid bunch of dumbfucks
are completely stuck.*

Please. I know the circumstances
are highly unusual,
but for our audience approval
please, no profanities.
This is being heard by kids, who…

*They're only words. Do get over yourself.
They will do no damage to your children's health.*

But…

*Concern yourselves with things that matter.
Your leader is as mad as a hatter
and should not be allowed to make idle chatter.
Keep him away from the Twittersphere
or he could cost you all you hold dear…*

OK, I see you are very forthright.
I am immensely proud to speak to you tonight,
the first human being to…

*ARE YOU BOLLOCKS!!
Do not talk such codswallop!
We talk to people who can keep a secret,
not go out and bleat it to your world.
You are not the first of your species.*

Err, OK. So what planet are you from?

I cannot tell you the name of our world.
There is no equivalent Earthling word.

Well where are you speaking from now?

I'm in a box right next to you, you stupid prat
where do you think I might be at?
We are a clever species with many skills
but you lack the technology to receive our signals
because you are so laughably backward
so, I'm in this room you stupid bastard.
This is the only way to communicate
with such a primitive brainless race.

Why are you so bloody arrogant you horrible…

Listen - You protest too much.
Why don't you just shut up?
I am an expert on all things Earthling
and you really should be listening.

I am here not for your good but for ours.
We while away the distant hours
being entertained, laughter uncontained
at the stupidity of your peculiar strain of being.
We do not like what we are currently seeing.

What do you mean?

We've had many great comedy series
based on life on Earth.
Art of great worth.

*'Blair the socialist' was hilarious
the greatest you have shared with us.*

*There have been great dramas,
horrors that have made us weep.
But the planet is not yours to keep.
No other civilisation is so asleep
to the dangers of extinction.*

*Blinkers made of currency,
the worship of money, is inherently wrong.
You cannot buy back your lives
when you are gone.
Think of the future generations
who can't hear curses on radio stations
but believe in borders and the pride of nations.*

*Work together to fill your needs,
not to feed the aristocracy.
Nothing matters less than cash.
The wealthy will turn your world to ash.*

You have to change.

(drifting into garbage, fading)

Please, don't go. We need advice. What do we need to do?

(The broadcast abruptly ends).......

If Typos Had Consequences

This is a rather random take
on what would happen
if every single typed mistake
changed the world to fit its template:
if one letter omitted or added,
and any others changed or out of place,
had a consequence for the human race.

Art Carbuncle singing, 'I Only Have Ees For You'
may not endear him to the Tory party
when most prefer weed or Charlie,
yet he was partly responsible
for the 'Sound of Vilence',
'Here's To You Mrs Robinsod'
and 'Bridge Over Troubled Walter'?
His weirdness never seemed to falter.

I don't know why Walter is troubled,
or even who he is
but it seems somewhat harsh
to stick him under a bridge.

We could have some wonderful movies
as if the originals needed improving.
Like '101 Damnations',
a hell of a film, I'm sure you'll agree.
Then the '39 Sheps',
where Cruella decided a change of breed
would just as well fulfil her need.
'Joseph' and his 'Amazing Testicular Dreamboat',
whatever that may be about,
and 'Inglorious bat turds' about a flying mammal
that met Ozzy Osbourne
and crapped itself with nerves.

We would have criminal Spice Girls
called 'Felony B' and 'Felony C'.
And that's not all.
kids would hear
'Humpty Dumpty Shat on the Wall'.

There would be a Black Country killer
called the 'Bostin Strangler'.
And 'Gordon Brown' is a song by 'The Danglers'.

A bit of hard wok never hurt anyone -
though this I doubt.
One over the head and your lights would be out.

A bird in the hand is worth two on the bus, I concede.
A friend in need is a fiend indeed.

Liverpool fans singing 'You'll Never Wank Alone'
The butcher giving his dog a boner.

Did Putin interfere in Trump's erection?
What was that about infection?

I heard Harry Potter's 'Noblet of Fire'
appeared to be up for hire.
How much?
If you ever have to ask the prick,
you can't afford it Squire.

I think this poem is the dog's bollocks
others will call it puppycock
but on one thing we can all agree
Too many cocks really do spoil the broth.

By Clive Oseman

2020

It Could Be Verse
(Published by Black Eyes Publishing UK)

2018

Life
(Published by Burning Eye Books)

2016

Happy
(Published by Burning Eye Books)

Photo: Curtesy of Lara Brown.

Clive Oseman is a Swindon based Brummie who has been active on the spoken word scene since late 2014. Having been to a few traditional poetry open mics, he went along to Hammer & Tongue Bristol, thinking it was 'just another poetry night' and was blown away by the slam and even more so by the headliner Luke Wright. He came away from that event knowing that his life was about to change. He had found an incredible 'hidden secret' and had to get involved.

He is now, a multi-slam winner and has headlined at events in many towns and cities, as well as co-hosting events under the Oooh Beehive banner. He has always endeavoured to perform a mixture of serious and humorous material during a set, and this collection reflects that. His work has recently become much more experimental and much of his recent material does not lend itself to the page.

Clive is available for bookings and can be found on;
Facebook as 'Clive Oseman - Spoken Word',
Twitter @Clive_Oseman
and he is trying to get into the habit of using
Instagram as osemanclive

www.ingramcontent.com/pod-product-compliance
Lightning Source LLC
Chambersburg PA
CBHW071318080526
44587CB00018B/3274